Love is Light

love is light

Published by love is light, 2024.

LOVE IS LIGHT

First edition. February 25, 2024.

Copyright © 2024 love is light.

ISBN: 979-8224285761

Written by love is light.

we have to, be some where, i am here, now i am
i found thyself, in all will, to expand in, for ever more
source essence love, light will reach, every one through, all us
together

we are there, destiny fate freewill, to be one, for all ways
soon with are, earth humanity collective, galactic community womb
i am it, self i am, thy self i, am are selves

afraid being tricked, becoming lost from, real true natural, core self
source
not any more, or every less, than each other
for one another, in are love, with light together

false in ception, real en caption, true re citation, evoke ex citation
am be coming, wonderful beautiful magnificent, clear pure true,
embrace are family, to thy self, as one being, serve other selves

sense different selves, source natural virtual, child youth elder, merge
en whole
work the construct, once you knew, your really are, love in essence
hold a tool, in your hand, materialize your creations, make them
matter

are made up, of energy in, the here now, you and i
get to know, love in essence, how you love, it self less
take some time, get to know, love in essence, how essence exists

is being a, bee as thy, to imbue nourishment, in thy deeds
relate to construct, the tool in, with all form, in harmony with
layers to all, mind body spirit, core template astral, parallel timelines
universi

capable re inventor, yourself again and, each new moment, there is
opportunity
such is infinity, potential and possibility, i have faith, we will be
drawn together with, our tool pen, this universe works, in a trinity

essence tool creation, co-creation with, reflection of the essence, imbuing energy together
    even though they, are reflections does, not make them, any less real
    you are there, reflection after all, if between is, pure crystal clear

will be one, in a sense, on a journey, ascending to oneness
    view point change, acknowledging everything has, to pass thru, hub prism nexus
    our own filter, lighten in load, as time passes, we answer the

call from light, to the feel, of oneness and, inner harmony realm
    it becomes you, our whole world, to share open, and with freedom
    a new earth, full of abundance, bright balance esteem, unique equal perfect

multifaceted multidimensional beings, now is time, to access more, who you are
    make decisions consciously, moment by moment, free from all, sub conscious programing -daniel scranton
    unite co-create together, key to portal, family of cosmos, joyful exciting bliss

tune in to, one and another, to their reality, because you are,
intention with purpose
    higher self conceives, physical brain receives, mind perceives in, ego
interprets with
    call of spirit, is with in, bring are light, summon our love

open gate way, in thy self, be as one, all that is
    with inspiration to, inspirit another spirit, and inspire the
    be like water, let it flow, in and go, to have clarity

maintain balance stability, love with light, other harbor relate, presence
with difference
    i am the moment and each new moment for divine purpose
    meet the new, light unconditional love, that emerges within

me and others, around me from, day to moment
    potential the light, that sees all, and feels tide
    in to alignment, with the flow, of are lives, to thrive alive

benefit of medicine, allows me to, balance on plateau, rather than peak
    i wont be, as phased by, lower vibrations directed, toward my aura
    bubble to surface, gently felt give, compassion for sensitivity

to where i, find and point, my self for, better or worse
    carefully ween off, my crutch and, behold all and, thy response ability
    to be deliberate, and conscious in, my choices and, respond as positive

we can be, in each others, company with out, agreeing with a, hot button topic
    we are with, are source becoming, whole gem crystal, myriad sparkle jewel
    balanced is centered, align with gift, flow higher self, through are nexus

heart is given, divinely and purposefully, for lower selves, extend your hand
    for the gift, we receive in, people need it, as you did
    beholder of boundless, light an extension, of your self

know ties to, ties in tide, in ties tie, aspect of tide, with higher self
    do feel right, for give in, beliefs i have, for my future
    know which lies, behind hidden meaning, with in words, in the
whole

in the broader, picture people say, and you say, love and light
    to balance center, integrate that aspect, be source in, all that is
    clear and open, conduit to channel, the neutral point, with out
condition

jynx is your, choice to feel, doubt or grasp, to your truth
    still in that, clears and illuminates, assumptions and lies, they rise up
    let go of, fear there is, not a problem, until you make, one out to

change is from, one point of, spectrum to another, flow is vast
    gentle guide embrace, it spirals upward, with us as, part of us
    balance your strive, to thrive in, divinity and honor, when you do

absorb channel emit, say think feel, hold grasp posit, and let go
trust the whole, unfoldment of reception, two way contact, to re unite
re crystalize your, higher self connection, with source in, writing action voice

trust it is, malleable encompass harmony, i am position, myself in moment
see them as, harmony and give, them your initial, heart felt thought
focus direction first, with honor place, your attention on, their unconditional love

give no meaning, wont have one, do not worry, knot knowing or
having to give, some thing up, feel and see, with what you
know now about, our present connections, and momentum forward, relax and ask

what do i, know my best, self would be, if from calmness
look at the, trust you already, have for thyself, in here now
truth will become, shrouded in fear, from imbuing it, with negative judgment

maybe there are three main paths to the center and to each other, view, feeling, and inspiration
I am doing beautifully
Not supposed to be of service, choose to be

You can tune into your own world if your feeling too uneasy at the moment with your outside or tune into the light in every moment if your feeling uneasy with your inner world. Once u acknowledge and see it, them and yourself free of fear, full and whole, momentous and true

Perfect is not perfect, each choice you choose is good enough to be perfect in sources eyes. source does not see a problem in letting you choose, source does want to join you and you to join in our choices as one. Source chooses all, to gather in, one by one

There is always a positive and neutral and balanced way of looking and feeling about someone or a circumstance or situation

You can trick yourself to un tricking your self, that is perfectly empowering for u to give yourself that permission. in fact there is nothing that is not a key a to a new door of re-membering and becoming a conscious and lighter and loving creator being, choosing harmony and unity when they prefer it, and are ready for it to become more of a part of you

We expand up like and upside down pyramid, and from that expansion generate a broad point of view from the peak that is like a north facing pyramid and we and our hearts reside in the center of that existence of that Merkabah, and we expand in 6 directions, connecting every way in the realm

Source wont let anyone hide or run forever, with each moment and life we live, source moves you gently forward and up readying you to take the wheel.

There is at least a little bit of dark or door presenting it, with the greatest light, and at least a little light in the deepest darkness, and everything in between, nothing to fear being far from true center. Your will to stay near to your and each others heart will be supported and sent along with our hearts.

Face what ever is in the way of facing what really is, let go of what or how it must be, and let in unity, divinity, trinity

It is perfectly valid to copy preserve and archive. Its you demonstrating your direction and momentum, it is you birthing in to thyself and thy creations. Its okay to demonstrate what feel benefits yourself as each other as a whole, tuning into your intentions and call to intentionally extend to connect where we meet to gather each member of our soul to feel calm and free of mental gymnastics, Focus on the calm still flow of fullness, and let go of your gravity towards chaos and measurement

dark one or light? one creation or multiple? we are the light in the dark, i am all ole and not just all one, i light are love in each other for one another, as we dance with are rhythm to draw closer in are selves with the other, dancing with are soul in creation. we can give are hearts to are other, and one another, in faith, trust, and knowing, they will feel its warmth as you do in are co-creation.

trinities. Maybe i can apply this to my mind and mental pursuits and gymnastics, and to my received gifts and given gifts.
concept intention relation, actions surroundings people

What is the concept or meaning i give out or in
What is the intentions i give
How do i relate to thy gifting

No answer is needed, we are the solution, the sol union
        the ole ocean within the drop
        there is always, a way out, of the dark

breathe and seek, love and light, to the eye
        knot need focus, on the dark, you are free
        crystalize and dissolve, with each breath, in every moment

become the great, love in dark, trace the light, yin and yang
        everyone else is, in each other, with one another
        tie each moment, together their change, in there emotion

i think people become liking pain and guilt, to feel proud to a-void their or their loved ones feeling of pride in fear that they might be right in the situations they faced are wrong, unworthy, and violating. i seek the pride i have in me and my families life and can summon. i am proud of everything and every step we give to ourselves and demonstrate one to another and lift each other back up to center. i meet my higher self and triangulate my center to be in 5 dimension. to re-invent your self but not disconnect from your lower selves. there is also two more paths to the center of it all, connection and freedom.

we are the meeting, the meeting in the middle. where are hearts and soul always remained, that is what and who we really are and already are, we are as special as that center with each other is

trinity, your lower self the trace of void, and your nexus your heart, and your higher self and all 3 as a ole is your source self

the dark symbolizes i am changing, worse to better, for are transforming with light

i am the dark or the light in the truth

This is How You Stretch & Bend Time ∞The 9D Arcturian Council, Channeled by Daniel Scranton

"Greetings. We are the Arcturian Council. We are pleased to connect with all of you.

We have an abundance of time on our hands, because we have no limitations when it comes to time, and because we have no limitations when it comes to time, we get to be timeless. We invite you to experience yourselves as timeless, even though you do still use clocks and calendars to keep track of things there on planet Earth. Yes, it is easy for us and challenging for you, but you went to Earth because you like challenges. You are not trapped there, and you are not there only because you've created karma with other people. You are there by choice, and you make that choice because you do love a challenge.

When you have less of something, like money, you have to stretch it. You have to make every bit of money that you have count, and the same is true when you feel as though you have certain time constraints upon you. When you feel that you have less time, then you need to be even more present in the time that you do have in a twenty-four hour day. That is how you stretch time; it is by being very conscious of each and every passing moment. It is by making the decision of what your relationship with time will be. If you want time to move faster when you are in a traffic jam, then you have the ability to do that. If you want to move faster in the completion of your ascension, you can do that as well. If you are enjoying a moment in time, you can stretch that out and have it feel like it is longer than it actually is. Time does not have to fly when you are having fun.

You get to work with time in the same way you get to work with every concept, every idea, every vibration, every emotion, and every thought. That's what you are there to do. You are there as creator beings to use what you are given as your raw materials. Time, believe it or not, is one of those raw materials, and so is money, and so is love. Bring more love to everything that you do and infuse that love into it, and you will have no issues with time whatsoever, because you will be in love with whatever you are doing and with whom you are doing it. Love is always the answer. Love is always the secret, and you can feel more love when you are more present.

When you are more present, you are more grounded and you are more heart-centered, and therefore you are more likely to feel that love that is your true self, your true essence. Make time your friend, your tool, and your assistant, and that's what it will be for you. Do not fear the future, and do not have regrets about the past, and you will also change your relationship to time and to the present moment, which is where all of your power is and where all of the love is.

You are timeless beings of love and light, and this ole life experience is but a blip in the realm of eternity. And so, we invite you to remember that as well the next time you are stressing out over time. Remember that your infinite and eternal nature is always available to you when you tune in to your heart.

We are the Arcturian Council, and we have enjoyed connecting with you."

i open center, lead lower self, separation to connection, dissonance to harmony
    when they rise, and meet there, centering of our hearts joining as one
    more i rise, meet opportunity of, moment in all

the more my magnitude becomes my, draw to embrace my other selves
    we are unique, we share are uniqueness with each other and one another
    three main paths, trust to center, we meet together, connect our paths

what you die down, to reach oneness
    what you hear to to feel together
    what you vie with to hold tride

what you express to call forth
    their the heir, there the here
    i choose to use this tool in love for myself with all

choose to check, choose are ready, chose with love
choose be steady, choose with freedom
adorably cute, beautifully sweet, magnificently awesome

edit out from time, change is here now, expand in to already
    choose from remembering dark and light, fear with love in light
    choose in remember all timelines, parallel realities, multiple
dimensions

choose remember stillness, moving, excitement
    give up, my connection in, form with formless
    feel our hold, love in essence, reach for freedom

your supposed to, be afraid fear, itself and power
    do knot need, to be at, the same time
    once your naught, afraid of yourself, you let go

let them go, trust your will, reconnect with equality
meet their darkness, with are light, let you go
with trust in, receive are center, connection with in

17

behold are love, enlighten space around, us as one
am seeing our, service in experience, of thy self
with each other, and one another, in shared experience

receive the call, give complete faith, in us as, we are they
you do knot, need to be, afraid of growing
lets see how, we find our, selves in tomorrow

i do knot, have to hold, to my specialness
let it go, and trust i, can be one
with in all, eternal in equality, infinite with luminescence

the sacred I, the sacred you, the sacred us
behold them in, heirs true form
nothing wrong with, resin of life, can be resolved

with are spirit, you channel in, around and out
    i am equal, to them all, you and us
    crawl with limbs, climb step in, connection with transformation

am higher self, to lower self, center are equal
    can be heir, in center reach, through the air, for lower selves
    let go of, what is heavy, about the local, family core layer

connect them equally, and as equals, as you expand, with next layer
    proud of all, energies and connections, we have joined, into are realm
    it gets easy, better every day, tracing the doubt, from out fear

it is The, doubt and fear, as it is, knot of Are's
naught the center, it does knot, belong to us
be long for, us all to, stem center to

all vibration we, activate are channel, from within creation
   attend each step, as we traverse, closer to harmony
      i trust, i triangulate us, i true our contact, treat your energy

to are truth, means open wide, to ole flow, of it all
   we can slow, to a crawl, to the stillness
      of unconditional love, i all ways, love for you

one aspect in one hand, and another in each other
   relate are co creation for co create are relation
      we clear canal, for are birth, from no thing, in to everything

we are honing, are navigation of, each realm with, frequency of
vibration
    i trust i, am held safe, free in you
    connect and grow, hone your trust, in all unknown

attend their trust, let them attend, mine in them
    et's, my self and, my loved ones
    for give and, let go of, power and wisdom

trust in others, and be fulfilled, that your will
    fill each other, up and be filled, by one another
    full by all, higher non physical, beings of source

flow down love, light flow up, we are flow
    thank you all, my selves in, my nexus being
    there for me, in any choice, intend with all

there is lot, of crystals in, all of us
respond equally to, their gifts for, you and us
for there connection, and interaction with, in the all

roles are powerful, it all swirls, with in me
there no week, month and year, all ways today
search lower selves, for buds for, thy seed nourishment

the deep below, the ice berg, tip above water
side streets everywhere, may find yourself, not in know where you are
that is when, reach for depth, and meet center, wonder trust
connection

move gently through, share slowly with, kindle love kindly
generate a vortex, become a genie
connect are extension, and let nourish, in and forth

join your child and crawl with source
join your youth and coast from heart
join your elder and cruise beside soul

express your energy, allow it to, flow out safe
    open and free, into the open, with in freedom
    reach for them, and give them, opportunity to reach

there are bathrooms, in the fifth, dimension in universe
    see you on, in every moment, will to discover
    from color we, heart with events

there are seeds, in our past, stem to source
    cant remove past, it close present, seed to plant
    united divining trinity, are approach in, alignment with creation

there is stuff, at the bottom, that is different
and very good, perhaps are past, friends and family
until we all, become part of, the wind that

be long for, us all time, side in tide
    guide navigate wonder, behold unfold emerge, humor art events
    hold them beloved, and dear as, they hold lie

higher vibration in, center balance neutral, better for everyone
    give over form, rise up meaning, important to life
    let go force, give in purpose, trust with creation

lay down from, are spirit near, heart rooting for us, with loving light
    expire from dark, respire out fear, inspire in love, transpire with light
    i must have, your suppose to, why do we

trinity, true no ties, tide with harmony
ride the wave, of love in, the every moment
will acknowledge fear, when i am, scared to let, out my light

flow love in, with all light
open my eyes, feel in hearts, love are light
with love for, i my self, you are free

my self is, in are nexus, with all source
fear in dark, belong knot mine, unconditional love all
back step once, we are in, step forward already

revolve with orbit, evolve like shaman, involve to gather
look both ways, reverse easy enough, work naught anymore
compassion forgiveness embrace, service is beautiful, sovereignty is
miracle

i thy self, and other as, open work up
clean the sink, with are spirit, let it drain
notice all magnitude, let it go, with flow out

investigate a new, speaker and radio, voice and tune
be lenient with, all your selves, for we seek
with love in, gift we member, gift light inspire

we let go, of the illusion, with in freedom
we receive with, love in light, in all radiance
we become are, essence of seed, plant of master

we safely traverse, with true trajectory, in hope full
we open up, to receive in, love with light
illusion condition fusion, relationship with self, blade share soul

negative feel pass, naught moving on, allow all by
dark is free, from in us, being are friend
here and now, they wait for, are meal together

we serve for, attendance with are, love in light
people on edge, look far away, from appearing short
close lies draw, center to gather, flow up inspire

fear i let, go from soul, in to void
i bless existence, with are heart, we gather in
i emerge with, are source in, love with light

i play today, moment by moment, and let in, heart felt guidance
creating a sound, conception of existence, with here now
i we tri, each new day, let in inspiration

giving are selves, balance we need, thrive and alive
the dark pass, light join in, complete are heart
connect in point, draw out dark, bring all love

moment in us, with are faith, trust and know
in are vortex, orbit around us, from always we
with are self, return equal energy, invite balance dance

light a way, feel are change, to join harmony
i let synchronicity create as one
apple of eye, eden of sanctuary, eve with in

feel pure joy, draw up with, wisdom gratitude enlightenment
write in gratitude, call are soul, love light union
draw up wisdom, united we write, with grateful divinity, call soul
trinity

knot afraid of, either side in, to know all
will balance with, heart body soul, connection with in
new chapter in, are here now, with every one

grateful for appreciation, wave with in, are selves united, divinely in one
　　are channel is, clear in are, love with light
　　hold in subtlety, be elevated love, create are shine

whistle bell call, existence horizon essence, infinity with eternity
　　i know it, is beautiful in, are own way
　　let go and, join to gather, rem in mer

there is infinity, from us here, eternally encompass, all are selves
　　trust in listen, hold are heart, guide to moment
　　let it out, with faith in, embrace for compassion, with in forgiven

are one with, in every one, in all link, with are time
relate in moment, elate in sync, elevate to gather
will be with, you forever and, all ways nearby

matrix in seed, are eden with, joy to born, love with light
	i thank you, for guiding are, light in dark
	we are one, now and here, welcome in joy

imbue known attribute, human collective consciousness
	i gladly revise, and save progress, thy self permission, for hero mission
	with up ward, flow with in, are co creation, in source grace

to view with, in revision we, synchronize are pendulum
	we are one, here in now, welcome with joy
	know thing between, you and us, in side are, aura field resonance

with are radiant, source with are, brilliant star light, in the truth
i take out, orders for give, in are boarder, within are elder
for shame guilt, fear of miss, treatment of are, dignity with in

embark outside of, our self in, thy self for, are selves within
i am the, love in are, essence horizon existence, in to we
source shining out, what matter is, who you are

in touch with, love in who, i step in, to become with
are brilliant light, encompass are way, in are hearts, song and dance
you are a, ruin explorer for, a way shower, into the unknown

selves for a, better tomorrow and, a bright future, with each other
free from skating, on ice to, follow through are, intuition to begin
i am you, and me in, are love with, in true light

pure and innocent, beyond be leave, we are members, of are selves
from am all, and no thing, in all with, in all us
eternal in appreciation, infinite in gratitude, one with you, all with
one

we pour are, heart and soul, into each other, and one another
in are sacred, flame of desire, and passion felt, by are source
to drive further, than any before, or ever will, to connect in

our way home, where are family, live with each, other in all
save change for, peace in prosperity, in divine interventions, contact
with in
are ole union, transfixed on dance, with in emergence, of are source

to gather with, all of are, selves once again, and now forever
in spire up, to be come, beholden in are, heart to humor
subject is known, and unknown in, are object of, interest in time

deject are condition in are attachment to your self is steam
traject in to are open arms in all embrace with all gates
drink from are, well of opportunity, in to unity

dig deep down, to bedrock where, we lay down, to rest with
    in search for, hidden treasures above, and beyond for, all to discover
    to return to, gemstones and crystals, for every single, brother and
sister

and bring about, a new way, of life with, equality and joy
    in heart and, body with soul, summon manifest create, with in all
    one at time, all time one, in bright are, sight for light

all in love, with love for, each other and, one and other
    for are ole, matrimony blessed with, are heart in, all thy love
    we press on, the dial with, pulse with in, friend we are

in are journey, to the call, of the cosmic, in your vortex
creation to the, temple within kingdom, come on crown
fission permission mission, experiment in side, be a live

did you leave, a tip in, gratitude towards each, other in together
    for ever as, one being true, greatness in one, and an other, with our
unity
    for us to, unfold as part, of one and, another as divinity

in our seek, for all love, in connected truth, in our night
    believe you me, trust in us, place faith with, in are heart
    that we will, get a long, reunion in peace, with grateful excitement

why did you, well come done, for give us
    we will be, with you in, no time here
    for us to, say good bye, my lovely light

a world at, peace from fear, clarity in dark
we sew together, piece by piece, stitch by stitch
weaving together are fine tape story instilled on film

birth are children, freedom and freewill, to be alive
    in are flame of compassion and gratitude we burn in side
    to light ways to are heart of eager joy

in ever new, here in now, moment in twined
    to the journey, of are lives, soon to come
    welcome fruits of, are labor of, love with light

stay and born, a new life, tender sweet love
    with in staged, attendance are audience, mom in heart
    from the depths, i evoke love, with light in, harmony with balance

subject is known and unknown in are object of interest in twined
the future is not set in stone, i remember are direction up together
in spire with spirit, everything as everyone in everywhere

35

we are in, the here now, we are one
    find your way up as unity with divinity in trinity
    may your dreams be full of joy and loving light

as we become more and more fulfilled in trust with source
    as are true natural core self, center equal balance
    with all aspects of yourself, all aspects of source

its all in are roots toward skies, in are shine towards home
    be loving and, gentle with your, ego as we
    find are own, way of opening, up and letting, go are future

is not set, in graved stone, always be reborn
we are like water in change, inner phase equal are outer phase
emerging interactions initiated, by thy soul, meeting in agreement,
best for all

erode factory scaffolding, emerge co creation, expand in all
search i am, each moment now, summon energy memory, remember
in now
look to future, with all we, will have together

sought help because, was unsure about, creating my future
from the present, it serves me, to feel good
listening to music, using my computer, feeling in to

who i am, past in now, to are future
look at positives, equality and neutrality, of the present, moment
with unity
search with in, to relieve my, feeling of crisis

of negativity with, being unsure of, creating my future
search within me, again and again, to remind me,
of these things, who i am, with all feeling, sacred with divinity

another victory in, one are goal, break tie free
  walk to park, chat in spark, art are part
  let program go, from are record, in to alive

resolve my point, dissolve our joint, solve are anoint
  master your wonder, wonder your master, your wonderful equal
  close to home, yet so far, i am you

everyone goes through, these trying times, joy comes in
  every one nest, tiny or tall, bird begin flight
  board the ship, chart are course, remorse in source

garden of life, flavor and spice, soul is magic
    from sun down, to sun rise, everyone directs day
    horn in heart, we cymbal are, conductor in concert

gate in station, all connected lines, meet in here
    board a train, see where you, will end up
    seat with in, your hearts cabin, view with in

we are safe, with each other, one an another
    brush against heart, paint of intention, felt soul momentarily
    trust in faith, we know what, are destiny is

hold loving space, between are selves, and another encounter
    integration is necessary, have your desires, create what you want to
manifest
    and have a rich inner world, that leaves you complete and fulfilled

every time you enter it, everything is the one
be twin lies, be leave story, know thy self
fear my lost, every one with, found in here

it is the, consciousness of humanity, that matters most
    times are perfect, achieving balance in, your selves lives
    choosing what you, think about and focus on

i am before, am here now, i am present
    we are equal, to are source, with in us
    remember are heart, gather your self, remind for spirit

it is okay, to become complete, and be new
    no shaken awake, no flooded awake, no vulcanoid awake
    release anything everything, not serve you, at this time

times of doubt, you want this, right on track
master i am, with in source, for are order
let go surrender and trust

activate, release, transform
    loss, abandonment, fear of unknown
    handle with more, grace trust faith, in who and, what you really

are as source, energy beings of, all that is
    i am the, flow with in, all for one
    i am present, for best intention, shared with self

i am in, the ole honest, truth in light
    i am all, and even more, with every one
    i feel my warmth and shine dawn till dusk

i thought i followed my excitement, which it was actually anxious
fear
    i know more who i am, love light with in all source
    press to close, lift to open, born to be, alive and thrive

cosmic are womb, rain bow brite, starlight with twilight
    winter of camp, beach have fun, peace in space
    swim in ocean, drive the highway, glide with wind

mine are cave, till in soil, fly thy sky
    train in transit, vibe with love, light are life
    moon with wane, sun in pride, star free gift

silence of love, will find spark, in live light
    enhance in music, rise up joy, beacon through night
    pyramid fore sight, view with feel, connect inspire freedom

compete in endurance, escape to solitude, rise in number, vibrant
with quest
    jade our contrive, forget the time, remember are lives, seek in surprise
    eject your disdain, secede from tango, gather all selves, connect with
love

die the dark, let go pain, born a new, free in will
    order in source, imagine co create, magic with light
    door and key, here and now, kingdom temple metropolis

heaven are hell, hour in hand, divine with time
    story in joy, with all source, tride in tide
    find with receive, are set for, spike of life

king and queen, fateful are encounter, draw with love
    summit from destiny, passion in desire, choose to create
    unite in harmony, forge are soul, life after live

order love flow out with in flux light source
tall with short, small in big, deep and high
let go of, anything that is, resistant in nature

43

bounty are forest, pure thy fountain, miraculous with mirror
beat your drum, sing in tune, rhythm are ride
bell ring nigh, choir call forth, band play orchestra

birds chirp in, delight with heart, sooth in soul
draw gate open, meet other companion, unite divine harmony
frolic in garden, dance the hall, celebrate are life

vow with voice, shift in momentum, grant thy god
valor are favor, mid with peace, trough way show
sail into sunset, buckle in adventure, voyage with prosperity

sacred thy jewel, glitter in gem, castle with crystal
pearl in mystery, gather each shard, seek to shape
staff of skull, love are mother, carriage all spirit

mine the earth, sun source shine, moon are space
    compass in commute, emerge with magic, foretell each fortune
    focus are aim, true in sight, light house beacon

portal with paradise, merge are source, live with life
    immortal in destiny, conscious in conscience, eternal are fate
    full fill in, serve thy self, all for one

restore are part, in moment we, remember thy piece
    sync with soul, unite divine tride, conduct with conscience
    manifest co creation, here in now, compassion in flame

luminous in being, scene and suspend, dawn are chorus
release all held, let it go, receive in flow
fill up space, to feel again, knot tide tied

45

move are spirit, asleep wake up, tune with soul
    symbol in chord, channel in lumen, scribe thy poet
    sign with heart, embody are value, change in harmony

attendance in role, present on planet, direct with womb
    free to roam, graze thy glade, enjoy in spotlight
    ascend thy peak, raise are scope, twinkle as star

reinforce with mirror, inward are reflection, within are empathy
    seek to conclude, when commune within, heart body soul, council light spirit
    reunion in remembrance, of who you, are with in, purpose for harmony

current with event, root garden eden, from in are, approach with self
space with time, in tie with, tide in side, rise in duality
evolve with planet, grow with pen, transform in spirit, peer out
polarity

realize what i, am like to, be a lone, on my own
way in shower, with in bewilderment, of are wild, side in nature
next level soul, intwine in entanglement, block in download, face
natural pride

revision with in, vision in to, envision with thyself, facet with aspect
birth of channel, flow with outside, inward to be, novel are insight
transmission tune with, in to cymbal, sound of are, music with
sequence

perception with mind, receive in body, conception from soul, interpret
our ego
to reconnect within, remembrance with in, ole in rise, with in self
true intuition to, become a hero, for harmony with, in each source

texture are poem, symbol are word, cymbal are feel, guide are know
form in order, master with equal, source in energy, show as mirror
machine in person, virtue of planet, earth are tree, plant with seed

sign with experience, higher self resonance, alignment of vibration, heart
in frequency
    ladder in union, human in collective, galaxy in womb, universe in
parallel
    write thy song, sing are tone, jive with vibe, boogy with dance

angel in voice, nod with beat, rock in rhythm, rhyme to sway
    hybrid are spirit, touch are felt, mind body soul, connect through
synergy
    paint are enneagram, color in human, brush in stroke, pattern with
cognition

vessel for action, are challenge with, growth with connection, in self
esteem
    neighbor with friend, encircle in circumstance, pure in situation, we
alchemy in
    glow with luminescence, beam in shine, bright are light, house with
eve

source commune experience, tool relation scope, code order pattern, archetype aspect face

ego connection feeling, word meaning form, honor choice agreement, scion envision mission

unconditional spectacle person, member spectacular harmony, direction action aim, trix truth tride

attune align activate, heart body soul, united sacred staged, joy full play

cymbal chime channel, song script scribe, moment co creation, collective eternal expansion

vibration flow frequency, dance rhythm step, inward unison energy, infinite potential unknown

vortex upward spiral, desire passion bliss, angel gather light, multiple parallel dimension

tale tie tide, decision depiction disposition, instill enliven insight, mimic mime memory

journey toward magnificence, unite divine trinity, relief remember restore, constant change context

venerable reality bubble, family friend familiar, extra terrestrial celestial, limit less combination

pendulum etch podium, circle alchemy signify, attach equal virtue, value all selves

move emotion thyself, train track set, find feel fly, return ride home defuse illusion-all fear, being under control, out side in, to ward order

decouple in-equal shame, situation re-main same, rap up present, flow master full

depart personal-ity guilt, circumstance action habit, womb plant seed, in garden eden

feel movement in, moment with momentum, gather in spire, with re membrance

ascension through dimension, time less density, conduce enough space, channel more source

anchor sacred honor, cultivate lively hood, integrate heart vibration, with hertz frequency

lighten heavy load, free self esteem, summon higher guidance, seek inclusive reception

appreciate genesis code, grateful for gate, feel happy return, home seat member

change for better, alignment with need, purpose balance harmony, focus desire will

embark out side, convene in gather, group with spirit, intuit inward realm

activate alchemy transform, council in light, form music band, orchestrate feel sensitive

intellect sense imagination, summit seat cognition, different contra diction, one magic nation

vibration ground choice, action emotion thought, orientation
connection behavior, feeling knowing resonance
     we are love, light with in, every one too, gather twin member
     that is life, we live with, in another other, each in abundance

i am that, one i am, in all with, us for you
     to be free, and shine in, your radiant glow, far and wide
     in balance through, heart to mind, soul with body, compassion em
brace

be an angel, with are guidance, greater in power, with higher self
     through out time, space apart in, puzzle to piece, part being nature
     surprise in present, moment here now, to be come, hero with journey

un ravel mystery, peer the abyss, void to ole, one in all
     let go of, resistance in nature, harmony with hope, faith and trust
     track in movement, pass the baton, run with wind, re lay frequency

source are energy, being care full, to let everyone forgive your transgression

meta physical philosophy, spiritual crayon community, be compassionate to ward each other

heal my body, mind with sole, communicate for embrace of one another

statue for holiday, relax and enjoy, share warmth together, hold in hand

entrain your humanity, feelin each heart, free are expression, shine through out

melody song tune, receive harmony balance, present with choice, receive thy gift

above sow below, thru with in, feel for true core natural self

tale tone tide, trident truth trinity, remember, we are on same team

birth inn answer, change yet again, celebrate all emotion, they are precious

planet evolve route, cycle spiral travel, step with faith, shift all hope

destiny with fate, free in will, transform al self, align ready energy

recital center stage, present aboard collective, journey our way home thru ascension

experience have hat, love in present, in light forth, with higher power
    channel multi-faceted, dimensional energy mean, genesis harmonic
beam, with in stream
    eb with flow, each one as, equal order master, team with member

generational we are, influence let go, modify i shall, night thy hero
    feel in air, bask with breeze, still thy wind, here in now
    al ways next, step in place, help come in, thru physical doorways

can always refresh, your course to, nature al round, out through in
    add to equation, adjust in algorithm, moderate make up, be together
again
    alter out come, become your future, fruit hanging up, in are tree

of life with, each other on, are mother earth, freedom with liberty
    to trust are, faith in knowing, where we find, our self worth
    is to bee, or knot be, source energy being, sweet love sun

connect are colors join with rainbow bright in beacon wright as rain
bridge of connection with are other half of ole brother hood with
sense to elevate your self and be love freedom joy in creativity

53

of clarity with emotion in view point to see clearly now here
keys to this universal ascension in two way communication for open
contact
halve in fun energy mission harmony enter nexus hub too gather
center

let in angel of grace with grateful embrace to compassion for give
know when to, say no i, am knot in, the same boat
raise your esteem to be equal with each one of us all

collaborators in co-creation with life we be together with are wonderful
world
in beauty with belief we re leaf to are branch of wisdom
with are song we sing on stage with sound resonate harmonic
synchronicity

nurture all team unify realm evolve together energy always moving
to oneness
    technique help dream way path share heal receive play imagine raise
grow
    include higher perspective limit less potential infinite alround spiral
eternal flow source

trust in faith seek divine wisdom teach guide dance union embrace give
    u and i we are transforming alongside everyone else in all existence
    bee loved ones share are desire plan our future bask et revel

discover our flame twin em body dawn dusk twilight sun sight bright
    meet in middle cross path center angel stream vortex twirl sing
behold
    sound of song sung sweet heart hear our melody soft care gentle

mind your way with others thyself become one another for a moment
    soul mirror reflection movement momentum near all us now forever
and always
    body entwined art journey feel compassion join half life here all ways

we would never agree you are unworthy, so we choose not to
feel the difference, as you bask in that vibration, you will find
your self reaching for that good feeling place over and over again

role and responsibility facilitate positive belief inspiration and growth
peace and harmony
     between all moving parts with in thyself as a source energy being
     love light shine thru all eyes, each voice listen, spoke by ear

forthright and insightful in help for thyself as another mother and
brother
     aboard their ship with warm wind in are sail flowing true north
     as we chart a course for a magnificent and happily ever after

peace of mind serene and tranquil deep and far clear and still
     relief of soul release to relinquish let go and hold no more
     bliss of body joy with passion toy in game fun and excitement

i am feeling more courageous to connect connect connect with
source energy
       i feel my trust in faith as the universe unfolds to gather
       i give my self permission to be my true core natural self

i give my self to everyone as my self from source energy
       i am free to be who and what i know is true
       i am loved i am loving i am love source loves me

i love source as my self loves all as me as one
       source energy being of love and light shown in night at dusk
       rise with dawn light your lantern show to each other are spark

meld minds eye see each others point of view meet your self
       unify soul vison feel another's heart song sung with compassion and
forgiveness
       bond body emotion imagine how they think feel and see the world

i am a sprout growing from a seed in the earth soil
i love you i am loved we are one big happy family
i am ole i am complete i join the in holy matrimony

i am to big to fail, wild horses couldn't hold us back
	as i become more aware of my surroundings and who i am
	i can see clearly now the rain is gone with out obstacles

in my way i play as i may say i am i
	that i am i am i am that i am i am
	going above and beyond who i want to be and being free

of resistance judgement and fear know more of you bee all ally
	are soul to gather for divine dance of life in blissful joy
	as we make contact and bodies become one once again for eternity

i use tools and write to signify my current feelings and direction
with momentum of ascended masters behind me and more in the
wake
as the awakened collective raises the level of consciousness lead in
home

tune and tone with the cosmos leaf in feeling mesmerized with soothing
open portal to the fifth dimension bee vibration anchor for all
benefits
i give everyone permission to be them selves for thyself to bee

i respond with compassion and forgiveness for all involved from thy
heart
we share are nourishment with one another for each other team
member
we feel ourselves grow up thru the soil of are lineage timelines

as we become timeless all ourselves merge and synchronize alignment
kundalini conduit
flow in tranquil abundant peace serene for life of happiness and joy
manifest a kiss from your true love your twin flame ignite bright

carriages are drawn we are riding are way homeward bound by
destiny
    fate is calling us back in to bee with you once again
    i am hang drum in with everyone and aligning my energy centers

guiding my consciousness as i bee thyself for others sake as mine
    own free will it is yours for thy giving unto ones self
    i am love you are lovely we are loving each other more

and more each new day with every breath in all moments together
    silence be golden toning is bold singing for gold feel in mold
    i change the current and flow together as we rise to surface

raising are children with us too see the light shine upon stream
    of water carry in us up stream paddled by spirit of canoe
    home is where the heart lives meet alive friend thrive as one

you exist... you always have and you always will. you are eternal.

your fundamental nature that of existence (rather than that of non-existence)

you are a part of existence, therefore you are eternal just like every thing else

everything is here and now.

we are experiencing our consciousness thru a created filter of time space

creation of ours that allows us to experience expansion in linear fashion

the one is the all and the all is the one.

many people believe they are separate from the ole of the universe

other people, other worlds, gods, spirits, etc. by this definition feel outside us

what you put out is what you get back.

you are creating by getting back what you are putt in out

everything changes except the first four...

any darkness with in me may pass thru me to the other
side where are souls meet and greet each other with in time
and space for are heart to warm up each hearth of one

we are all valuable in our own way equally and unconditionally loved
by source energy being you and i am being love is light
we all have needs for more some less than others for another

lover of light to bright up the night sky for new tomorrows
faith in trust surrender your resistance seek a peaceful harmonic
serene sanctuary
sing dance and play together for re leaf enjoyment match to gather

evaporate your steam and bee all moments for timeless in here now
with in everyone on the earth with your universal galaxy family tribe
growing as one tree of cosmos blossoming with the flowers of life

www.ingramcontent.com/pod-product-compliance
Lightning Source LLC
Chambersburg PA
CBHW021351160726
47994CB00007B/2921